CONTENTS

Contradanse
(Old French Tune)

ARRANGED BY
N. HOVEY AND B. LEONARD

NOTE: This solo will provide an excellent introduction to a light, semi-staccato style of playing. Although the meter signature is given as 4/4 the performing tempo should be approximately MM 𝅗𝅥 = 80 (MM 𝅘𝅥 = 160).

In Minor Mode

N. HOVEY AND B. LEONARD

A rather broad, legato style is suggested for the opening section of this solo. The *Allegro* section from measure 28, however, demands a crisp, detached style except where slurs rule otherwise.

The *Moderato* should be played at about 96 quarters per minute, and the *Allegro* very close to 152.

EL 3126

Air and March

N. H. SEWARD

SUGGESTIONS TO THE SOLOIST:

Maintain good hand position for smooth slurs such as measures 1, 2, etc.

Notice that the notes in bars 3, 11 and 27 are the same but the rhythm is different. Count carefully!

Spiritoso means "in a spirited style." Observe the accents and play the other notes lightly.

In measures 36, 39, etc. The note to which you slur should be shortened as much as the following staccato notes.

Maestoso means "majestically." In this piece keep the same tempo but feel as if you are a king or a queen parading before your subjects as you play this section. Separate the notes slightly and maintain full tone quality. Use more breath for the accented notes. (Don't tongue harder!)

Reflections

N. HOVEY AND B. LEONARD

The opening section of this solo suggests a somewhat pensive mood. It should be played in a broad, cantabile style at about 108 beats per minute. Refer to your metronome to arrive at the correct tempo. At measure 25, however, the pace is quickened to about 126 to help imply a more joyful state of mind. Return to the original tempo at measure 41 and further diminish the tempo and volume in the final four measures.

Berceuse

BENJAMIN GODARD
Arranged by
N. Hovey and B. Leonard

Summer Holiday

N. H. SEWARD

SUGGESTIONS TO THE SOLOIST:

The first part of this piece should reflect the laziness of a summer holiday and should be played in a very smooth and singing style. Be particular about good hand position so that your slurs will be smooth. Move your fingers exactly together to eliminate "garbage" (extra notes) in the slurs.

Be careful of the change of key and time at 17. This section represents the happy, carefree playfulness of the summer holidays. Practice this slowly and evenly at first and then work up speed.

The dot at the end of a slur (measure 20, etc.) means to slur to the note and make it short and light.

A Scottish Air

ARRANGED BY
N. HOVEY AND B. LEONARD

Minuetto

N. HOVEY AND
B. LEONARD

At various periods in music history the *Minuet* has been known as a dance in slow, stately time . . . in rather fast, brisk time . . . and in a moderate tempo between the two. In writing this solo, the composer had in mind a speed of about 126 beats per minute. The soloist may wish to consult a metronome to approximate the correct pace.

When three unmarked quarter notes appear together in a single measure, they should be played exactly alike in length, with slight detachment. When two adjacent quarter or eighth notes are slurred, the first will obviously receive full value, and the second will be shortened slightly.
Following the above suggestions will help impart the lightness and grace implied in the initial term "con grazia".

Prelude and Italian Dance

N. H. SEWARD

SUGGESTIONS TO THE SOLOIST:

Finger C on the left following Eb in bars 2, 4 and 11.

Be particular about good hand position so that your slurs will be smooth. Move your fingers **exactly** together to avoid "garbage" (extra notes) in the slurs.

Be careful of the change of key and time at 13. This section is the "Tarantella" Which is a fast **Italian** dance. Shorten and lighten the second note of a slur and play the staccato notes very lightly.

Practice this part of the piece slowly with careful attention to notes, rhythm and lightness, then, **gradually** work up speed.

Cavalleria Rusticana
(Intermezzo)

PIETRO MASCAGNI
Arranged by Robert Lowry

HINTS ON INTERPRETATION ....

A RHD suggests to leave the Right Fingers down on the throat register notes for a fuller tone and smoother technic.

B Commas (9) indicate the end of a phrase for breathing. A dash (/) allows for a short "catch breath". All other breathing should take place during rests.

C This ornament may be simplified as:

D Even though the grace note appears under a slur, it is accepted practice to tongue it "gracefully".

E Play notes with a tenuto (−) mark their full value using a legato (soft and light) style of tonguing.

F The side Bb fingering will give a better tone in these instances where the right hand is not needed preceding or following the Bb's.

The Sioux Song and Dance

ROBERT LOWRY

*Perdendosi – Gradually decreasing tone and time.

Valse and Volante

EL 3126

Song and Prayer
(from the Opera "Hansel and Gretel")

ENGELBERT HUMPERDINCK
Arranged by Robert Lowry

FUN PAKS

simplified "Ensembles that Swing"
SOLOS, DUETS, TRIOS

Each book features four favorite tunes arranged especially for these instruments by JOHN FORD, outstanding composer/arranger for young concert band. FUN PAKS can be played as solos, duets, trios, or multiples thereof. A jazz/rock rhythm section accompaniment cassette is available to make the songs really swing!

FUN PAK FOR FLUTES
Book with Cassette (F3150FLT)
• Take Five
• Batman Theme
• Sleigh Ride
• On Green Dolphin Street

FUN PAK FOR CLARINETS
Book with Cassette (F3149CLT)
• Theme from New York, New York
• The Pink Panther
• Old Time Rock & Roll
• Have Yourself a Merry Little Christmas

FUN PAK FOR SAXOPHONES
Book with Cassette (F3148AST)
• Theme from Ice Castles
   (Through the Eyes of Love)
• 25 or 6 to 4
• Little Boy Lost (Pieces of Dreams)
• Georgia on My Mind

FUN PAK FOR TRUMPETS
Book with Cassette (F3147TRT)
• Theme from New York, New York
• Old Time Rock & Roll
• Santa Claus Is Comin' to Town
• Proud Mary

FUN PAK FOR TROMBONES
Book with Cassette (F3146TBT)
• Theme from New York, New York
• Old Time Rock & Roll
• Santa Claus Is Comin' to Town
• Proud Mary

All **FUN PAKS** are also available
without cassettes:
   Flute Book Only (F3150FLX)
   Clarinet Book Only (F3149CLX)
   Saxophone Book Only (F3148ASX)
   Trumpet Book Only (F3147TRX)
   Trombone Book Only (F3146TBX)

INSTRUMENTAL ENSEMBLES FOR ALL
DUETS FOR ALL • TRIOS FOR ALL • QUARTETS FOR ALL
by Albert Stoutamire and Kenneth Henderson

Any combination and any number of instruments can play together in harmony. Woodwinds, brass, strings, and mallet percussion (even snare drum in **DUETS FOR ALL**) can have fun playing in like instrument or mixed instrument ensembles.

The material covers a wide range of styles and music by composers from Baroque through contemporary eras.

DUETS FOR ALL and **TRIOS FOR ALL** range in difficulty from grades I through IV. **QUARTETS FOR ALL** range in difficulty from grades I through III.

The pages are laid out in an identical manner in each book so that performers can quickly locate a point for discussion or rehearsal. No page turning is required while playing.

This set of books meets the needs of classmates, friends, family and neighbors who wish to play together for festivals, concerts or just for fun. They are also excellent for learning ensemble playing, auditions and sight reading.

DUETS FOR ALL • TRIOS FOR ALL • QUARTETS FOR ALL fit your every need!
ALL BOOKS—CONDUCTOR AND PARTS—ONLY $5.00 EACH

 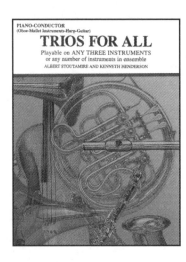 

DUETS FOR ALL
Stoutamire and Henderson

(PROBK 01337) **Piano Conductor, Mallets**
(PROBK 01324) **Flute, Piccolo**
(PROBK 01325) **Oboe, Guitar**
(PROBK 01326) **Bb Clarinet, Bass Clarinet**
(PROBK 01327) **Eb Saxes, Eb Clarinets**
(PROBK 01328) **Tenor Saxophone**
(PROBK 01329) **Cornet, Baritone T.C.**
(PROBK 01330) **F Horn**
(PROBK 01331) **Trombone, Baritone, Bassoon**
(PROBK 01332) **Tuba**
(PROBK 01333) **Snare Drum**
(PROBK 01334) **Violin**
(PROBK 01335) **Viola**
(PROBK 01336) **Cello & Bass**

TRIOS FOR ALL
Stoutamire and Henderson

(PROBK 01402) **Piano, Conductor, Oboe, Mallets**
(PROBK 01392) **Flute, Piccolo**
(PROBK 01393) **Bb Clarinet, Bass Clarinet**
(PROBK 01394) **Cornet**
(PROBK 01395) **Eb Saxes, Eb Clarinets**
(PROBK 01396) **F Horn**
(PROBK 01397) **Trombone, Baritone B.C., Bassoon, Tuba**
(PROBK 01398) **Baritone T.C.**
(PROBK 01399) **Violin**
(PROBK 01400) **Viola**
(PROBK 01401) **Cello, Bass**

QUARTETS FOR ALL
Stoutamire and Henderson

(PROBK 01435) **Piano Conductor, Mallets**
(PROBK 01427) **C Treble Instruments**
(PROBK 01428) **Bb Treble Instruments**
(PROBK 01429) **Eb Treble Instruments**
(PROBK 01430) **F Instruments**
(PROBK 01431) **Bass Clef Instruments**
(PROBK 01432) **Violin**
(PROBK 01433) **Viola**
(PROBK 01434) **Cello, Bass**

This music is available at your local music dealer.